Places of the Mind

Latosha Mitchell

Self-Published
ISBN 978-0-557-78967-2

Printed in the United States of America

TABLE OF CONTENTS

My Fair Cupid

I walked around with a disguise of a man
Who I'd thought might be the one for me
Who knew that with him, I'd feel lonely?
I was over shadowed by the mask he was wearing
While inside, my heart was tearing
So dark, I couldn't see
The monster lying here with me
So much pain
That my heart ripped completely
Felt like nothing existed
On the verge of giving up
I almost missed it
Cupid's arrow
Pierced me so deep
But I think it made me weak
Found love at last
With a man so true
But I wasn't able to win the battle I had with my past
So I withdrew
Not being able to give myself to him
Because memories reminded me of the one before
I drew everything out of line
I ignored the signs
"**SLOW DOWN**"
In bold letters I read
Instead, I went faster
Sped past the small print that said
"Impatience can cause disaster"
My heart was torn
And I wanted him to fix it
I pushed and pushed
But he wasn't the one who broke it
He never even saw it
Because with him I was heartless
I didn't take the time
To care about his needs
I just wanted him to satisfy me
But you can't be satisfied by someone who's not happy
So eventually he left me
Unhappily ever after
This tale seems unfair
My fair cupid
Is true love still in the air?

A Woman Scorned

Blinded by love
I fell for him
So deep was my love
The light so bright in my eyes
How could I not see?
Who he really was
I dared he was false
And trusted his love was true
When deep inside I knew
What he'd put me through
Yet I held on so tight
And fought with him every night
Still I couldn't let go
I tried, I know
To get away from it all
But I turn and he's there
To make sure I fall
Couldn't take it anymore
But I accepted his gifts
Though he's always out the door
Every night, a different shift
I knew he was lying
But I stuck by his side
"He's trying, he's trying"
The truth I denied
It had to stop
It had to end
I was engulfed in misery
But that was then

Blinded by fury
I packed up my anger
He didn't see that sign as he walked in
Marked "DANGER"!
Little did he know
That my patience ran low
I knocked him down to the floor
With one single blow
He knew I was pissed
And so was he
But no longer would I let,
His anger scare me
So I let him have it

With this torch in my hand
X marks the spot
Right there where he stands
As I throw down the torch
And cremate him on his land
I stand and watch him burn
Then put his ashes in the urn
For every violent man
Let this be a lesson learned
We as women
Bring you into this world
We as women
Can take you
Out of this world
Don't under-estimate the power
Of a woman scorned
For only your death
Will be left for all to mourn.

Signs

If he comes home at 11:30
Suspect he's doing dirty
When you know he leaves work at 7.
If he doesn't pick up the phone when you call
It's obvious he doesn't care at all
When he knows that upsets you.
If he sneaks in the bathroom to answer the phone
And he moans and groans
When you ask him what that's about
And he gets mad
Knowing you're his wife
That's sad.
If he comes home with make-up on his shirt
And he swears it's just dirt
Come on
What a jerk!
Or if he smells like soap
Because he just washed away the evidence
When he knows you know
That after working all day that doesn't make sense
How about when he clears his call log
And your mind is in a fog
Because you called him like a million times
Or when you find receipts from restaurants you haven't been to
He tries to make a fool of you
"Oh baby, you don't remember…"
Or when he starts to lack affection
You can't help but question
"Why"?
Or the married men who don't wear their wedding band
But want you to understand
It's so it doesn't get messed up at work
And e-mails
Oh hell!
He's cheating!
Everyone's been cheated on in the past
But you decide how long it lasts
The proof is in the signs
HE'S CHEATING!!!
But you already know.

Kiss

Wind blowing in my hair
The breeze gently caresses my body
I feel as if I'm not here
My body feels weak
My knees are shaking
The intensity I feel
Is making
Me vulnerable
To uncontrollable
Movements
As my right leg goes up
No longer acquainted with resistance
I'm in non-existence
With myself
Love has taken over
I'm drawn in by its power
The strength from it
I let it devour
My mind, body, and soul
Entangled in a web of desire
I feel the fire
The flames burn higher and higher
I start to overheat
I'm weak
But I yearn for more
Of this piercing sensation
Your body pressed against mine
My heart is racing
Trying to catch up to your love
So much, so fast
Each one better than the last
For future time and generations past
Nothing beats the timelessness of a great
Kiss.

Love me

What if I told you that I needed you?
To make me happy
And satisfy me
And I told you that I'll never leave
I'll stay by your side
I won't run and hide
What would you say to me?
Would you tell me all the things I want to hear?
Or say what's in your heart and be sincere
What would you say to me?

I want to know
Because I love you
And I want you
And need for you
To tell me
You want me badly,
Need me badly
I need for you to tell me how I feel,
Is how you're feeling too
Say you love me.
Say you love me.

Immortal Love

Our love is immortal
Bound by each teardrop shared
Creating a line of strength
Through weakness
We hold on
Through weakness
Creating a line of strength
Bound by each teardrop shared
Because our love is immortal.

Love Addiction

Distant we are
But so close to each other
Connected by our emotions
Physically incapable of sharing the same space all the time
Yet you occupy the space surrounding me all the time in my mind
I see you in my dreams in the night and the day
Dreaming away the urge to beg you to stay
Saying to myself that you will always be in my mind and my heart
No matter how long or far we are apart
But it's not enough
From every moment spent with you
My feelings for you get deeper
Causing me to want you even more
In turn making me weaker
Though caught up in this love addiction
Clear is my conviction
That it's not a phase.

Self-Esteem

I do not know you love
But you are always on my mind
People say you're hard to find
I would love to meet you one day.

I thought I knew you love
Long ago
You were tall and handsome
Romantic at times
You took me out
And wined and dined me
You were so intelligent
I wanted you to drip onto me love
I wanted to feel you love
I gave you power to take over my mental and physical state
I was helpless to you love, but then you told me I was nothing without you
And said I would amount to nothing
You blackened my eyes
You made me cry
Made me lose the baby I was carrying for you
Why?
If this is love
It's not what I expected
I allowed you to enter into my body
But from my body you were rejected
You sat around and watched me bleed
Bleed pain
From years spent with you
Losing trust,
Bleeding tears
From fear
Of no longer wanting to know love anymore
Not able to endure
I escape
From the harsh reality
That if I stayed
I might have caused a fatality of love
Although at the time
In my mind
You no longer existed
Until one day
I ran into an old friend of mine
Who I hadn't seen in a long time

She let me in on a little secret
That who I thought was love
Wasn't
Floored and stunned by the revelation so true
I began to realize
Indeed that wasn't you
But my friend knows love
She assured me I know love too
She said come with me
And I'll show you
She said love was around you the whole time
As crazy as that seems
And just in case you forgot
My name is Self-Esteem
So Self-Esteem and I
Went to see love
But no one was there
All there was
Was a mirror and a chair
And so I sat down
And stared into the mirror
And what do you know
Right before me
Staring back at me
Was a beautiful reflection
And so I said to it
Nice to meet you love.

CHILD ABUSE

Low self-esteem
But no one can tell
She hides in a soft shell
That can easily be broken
She has won the battles of life so far
But can't win the war with herself
She's breaking down
Afraid to go home
Even with her siblings there
She feels alone
Her mother's gone to work for the night
She goes to bed
To get ready for the day ahead
She can't sleep
Painful nightly reminders
Run through her deep
10:04 pm
Startled by the sound of keys turning
She closes her bedroom door
Maybe this time,
Maybe this time
He won't do like before
She prayed
And like a preying mantis
He preyed
The sound of running water
He ran for his teenage daughter
But daddy "I'm tired! Leave me alone!"
Cries go unheard
He bathes her
And tells her not to say a word
Scared and helpless
He dries her off
And helps her get dressed
"Go to bed", he says
"I'll come tuck you in soon"
Nothing she can do
But stare at the moon
14 years old
He goes to tuck her in
2 hours it took.
She cries herself to sleep

Thinking this can't happen again.
Saturday morning
While her step-dad is at work
She tells her mom everything that's been going on
The next few years were great without him around
Thinking life's better
Happily ever after
Until she found out they brought a house together
Stunned and confused
She wondered how that could be
Realizing now
Why she and her mom fought constantly
She was scarred with a tattoo on her brain
That read, "My mom chooses my step-dad over me"
She never imagined
Love could make you bleed so easily
Truth is there was no love
Spewed from her moms negative energy
Sad that in a crisis she couldn't turn to her own family
She was disowned and left with so much hate in her heart
Nothing mattered to her anymore
The pain she felt was rotting her to the core
She was stripped of her innocence
Stripped of her confidence
Hearing her mother preach about morals and independence
Became a bunch of mumble jumble that no longer made sense
Holding on to the pain was ruining her health
But she overcame her pain
And turned her sadness into wealth
Molested by her father
And feeling raped by her mother
This type of situation happens to too many
Of our young sisters and brothers
Afraid to say anything
In fear of their own
Growing up in a crowded world
Feeling all alone.

Who Cares?!

Since when did people not care anymore?
Sure, their were some
Unseen or barely there
But now people all over just don't care
How they dress,
How they talk,
What they do
To themselves or to you
Fashion has become a disaster
Modeled by unqualified idiots
Which I can't understand
Because it's not that hard to master
I walk around this prison playground
And watch all the immature thugs
With their pants hanging down
Showing their dingy boxers
Playing with their tricks
Who's only after a good dick
That's probably been through so many neighborhood bushes
It's going to take more than douches
To clean the nasty infection
Left from his erection
But these girls these days
Don't know about early detection
There are so many walking diseases
You have the "Pist. .. ", and the "hey ma" diseases
And the well known, "Yo shorty" disease
You have to watch out for
I can't take it anymore
Feel like I need to get out of town
But they're everywhere like the green grass
That grows all around, all around
Of which they smoke
And blow in my face and
All around and around
These inconsiderate fiends
Hang on the corners
And cause scenes
Up to no good
With no hopes of a better way
Because they're quote, “from the hood”
That's the same excuse June Bug used last week
The day before he was shot
But his brother just graduated college

And no one cares how far he's got
Because people are lazy
And are not trying to get up out the hood
Nowadays
Who cares about an education?
But hell
Why should they
When ignorance is sweeping the nation
I mean since when did tweeted
Become the past tense of twitter
I hate to sound bitter
But look
Between that and Facebook
We have new generation geniuses
At least they think they are
Because they keep daily reports/ autobiographies,
(Like who cares),
On these sites
And now they think they can write
I.D.K. what's going on,
Even though some entries make me want to L. O. L
It's no longer funny when kids grow up
Thinking that's really how you spell.
But this is what the world's coming to
No one cares
More and more people crying
Because there's more and more people dying
I'm constantly asking why and
I don't know why
Because no one hears me
So I try and I try
To make sense of it all
But there's no sense
In nonsense
And nothing will change
If all I have is ten cents
Due to this damn recession
But still money talks
And the more you have
The louder your voice is
So can someone please spare some change
To help me deliver this message"!

Caged Bird

Why does the caged bird sing?
Because he can't speak what's on his mind
Like a person who speaks of his vision
But can't see because he's blind
When one road is blocked
You go in another direction
As long as you reach the same destination
It's sad that you have to be limited
For the possibilities to be limitless
Makes me wonder
If the caged bird could talk,
Would he talk as much as he sings?
Or if the blind man could see,
Would he have a vision for anything?
Maybe it's better to sing and not talk
Or visualize and not see
For what you're incapable of
Might heighten ones curiosity.

Stuck

My head is aching
From thinking of you
All day long
That's all I do
I can't help it
I love you so much
I love your touch
I love your style
You drive me wild
I can't take it anymore
I want you so bad
But I can't have you
And that makes me sad
I'm in love with a married man
This I can't stand
Why you won't leave your wife
I can't understand
My friends think I'm crazy
I should have never been with you
But I was young
And had no idea how much pain I would go through
Now I'm stuck
In this situation
And all my frustration
Is getting the best of me
And it's making me angry
Angry at myself
Because I put myself here
And angry at the world
Because no one seems to care
But it's ok
That's what I want to say
But its not
Because I love you a lot
But I don't know why
When you won't leave your wife
I don't know why
When you tell me to get a life
I don't know why
I put up with your mess
And let you cause me so much stress
But maybe it's because
You tell me how much you love me
Maybe it's because

You say you will never leave me
Maybe it's because
Of all the things you do to me
Maybe it’s because
Of how you confuse me
I don’t know what it is
But I have to tell you this
It’s over!
It’s over!
It’s over!
But then I start to cry
And then it’s back on again
I can’t let you go
I can’t only be your friend
Damn!
I don’t think this will ever end
To be continued….

Who's To Blame? /Blame the White Man

We blame the white man for all our misfortunes
We're doing the best we can
So damn it! If all else fails
Blame the white man
Ignorance prevails.
Standing on long welfare lines
Trying to scrape for every nickel and dime
Yet with such hard times
We still find
The time
To have three and four kids
Chances for success decrease
Stupidity -like a disease, spread
Among our black people
Who read
From the mouth of a white man
How stupid we are
I ask –Whose fault is this?
The white man doesn't like the color of our skin
Angered by this we come together to fight him off
Only to separate because we don't fit in
Within our own circle of people
But we said everyone is created equal
Hypocrites we are
But the white man is to blame for us not getting far
Blacker the Berry the Sweeter the Juice
How about -Blacker the Berry the Harsher the Abuse
From outside and in
My own brother don't like the color of my skin
So now I have to change
So that I can fit in
Hold Up! Something isn't right
As I pick up the bleaching cream
To make myself more white
To be socially accepted by my brother and the white man
Who I can't stand
Might as well put the money directly in his hand
And we wonder why

The rich is getting richer and the poor is getting poorer
Something we will continue to hear more of
If the white man continues to have control
Yeah -Let's blame the white man
But aren't you sick of the same story being told
Now that Barack Obama is in control,
After setting a precedent
For being the first black president
There are high hopes for a dream that can possibly come true
But we will still walk around and complain
Losing sight of where to aim
And all I can do is wonder
Who's to blame?

Questions

To know true love
I'd have to read between the lines
To see what my very existence defines
Am I willing to go the extra mile?
And take on more than one can handle,
Am I needed like the flame of a candle,
When there is no power
Does my very existence continue by the hour?
Or has the sweetness of my life
Gone sour?
Do you treasure me, like I treasure you?
Do I make you uncomfortable?

Work of Art

Clearly defined by
Remarkable lines and figures that
Surrounds color, which
Gives off tones
Soft and hard
Evenly masked
I stare
What is this I find my eyes hard to shift from?
With Picasso and Leonardo
To my left and my right
I assume the picture in front of me is Starry Night
Because all I see are stars in my eyes
But I realize it's not.
The picture in front of me is far more worthy
There are no blues,
There are no yellows,
Just even shades of brown
Illuminating a glorious presence
In my eyes
The image chase my thoughts
And now I'm breathless
I'm left still and a fixated
Never another to have left me feeling this way
I must say
You are simply a work of art.

Dance

My minds at ease
Spirit is free
I feel the wind beneath my feet
As I jump and spin
To this hypnotic beat
Move left, move right
Jump up, Bend down
I follow this beat all over town
Neither here nor there
But I hear it everywhere
This beats in my soul
I lose all control
Joy surrounds me
The sound astounds me
I'm on cloud nine
Mind so clear
Stress behind
Left in the rear
Happiness fulfilled
With the art of dance
My escape from reality
When I get the chance
With power so strong
To move me along
Forever I'm tuned
To the beat of a song.

Purple

My favorite color is purple
When I think of purple I think of
Lilies growing
People singing
Along with the humming birds
Flying across the sky
I think of tomorrow
Of yesterday
Of today
I think of the way
The sun rises and sets
How the moon comes out at night
And the sun kindly re-positions itself
I think of that morning cup of coffee
The sweet aroma filling the morning air
The sound of my dreams
Calling to tell me the story
Of a girl whose favorite color is purple
Sweet purple addiction
I'm in love with you.

One Night Stand

I remember when
We went to the movies
And afterwards he took me out to dinner
We had such a good time
I stared into his eyes
He stared into mine
We took a nice stroll through the park
As we made our way to my place
I invited him in
We talked and laughed
And kissed
The way the French do
It felt like a fairytale
And just like that
I wanted the night to end well
And so it ended just the way I liked it
He was so amazing
And I was so relieved
My night and shining armor
Fulfilling all my needs
Feeling satisfied
I walked him to the door
We kissed goodnight
I never saw him again
Still sometimes I like to reminisce
About Mr. One Night Stand.

Time

Time waits
And stands still
Watching you
As you watch and wait for the hands on the clock to move
Breathe in
Breathe out
Tick tock
Tick tock
Time waits for you
To stop watching the clock

Untitled

Blind sight
Erased thoughts
Childish fantasies
Stolen memories
I fade with the times
I'm lost in translation
My words echo frustration
It takes time
It takes years
While the death toll rises
I roll with time
Until it leaves me behind

Convince

I have to convince myself
That it will be dark at night
And light in the day
That everything will be right
And things will go my way
But yesterday the light went into night
And the night was bright
Today is dark
And I feel tonight will be brighter
My anxiety builds
On top of my chest
700 pound weight
Weighing me down
I can't breathe
The air outside
I can't feel
Am I dreaming?
Or is this real
I should pinch myself
But whatever this is
Is pinching my nerves
Pinching my heart
Pinching my arteries
I'm falling apart
Try to convince me that everything is fine
That everything is right
Take sides with my mind
Help me win this fight
Convince me

Hair I am

Nappy head girl
Not keen to the press and curl
She’s freestyle with it, but
She wears it well
She’s fly and you can't tell her nothing

Straight head girl
Sleek, chic, smooth
See her confidence
In the way she moves
She’s fly and you can't tell her nothing

Kinky head girl
If she falls
She bounces back up
Got that kink in her step
She got it like that
She’s fly and you can't tell her nothing

Dreadlock girl
Survives without a comb or brush
Any altercation I suggest you hush
Because she’s fly and you can't tell her nothing

Bald head girl
Tough girl
Not afraid to show herself
To the world
She’s fly and you can't tell her nothing

Braid it up girl
You better stay in line
'Cause she can get ghetto
And still look fine
Because she’s fly and you can't tell her nothing

Afro girl
Firm with it
While representing a movement
She encompasses peace with her afro grease
She’s fly and you can't tell her nothing.

Girl, girl, girl

Do you girl
Wear your hair
According to how you feel girl
Rock, rock, rock
Rock that hair girl
Because we're fly
And nobody can tell us nothing!

Love Lost

I fell deep into his soul
So deep I almost drowned
My eyes became water wells
Overflowing into rivers
That flowed violently underneath me
I couldn't stop it
I couldn't scream
His silence was loud enough for the both of us
Still no one could help me
I was in too deep
We wandered in the forest of love
Happy as can be
Until I lost him

Untitled

Sometimes the driving forces of humanity and desperation
Are similar in nature in that
It seems as if you can't have one without the other
The other without one
Almost interchangeable
Often misconstrued with the concept of madness
Of which, it has less to do with
And more to do with
An internal sadness
Of which I believe
All humans possess
At one time or another
In which we desperately try to cover
For the sake of humanity
Or is it just me?

Dreams

Dreams are sweet sometimes
Kind of like a mango that's nice and ripe
A lingering imprint of someone else's lips against your face
A smile that stretches wide
The clouds comforting the angels up high
The angels before they vanish from those dreams
And leave us with reality.

To The One I Love

Your love becomes a times-table
Mirrored a thousand times over
As the days go on
Multiplying at every angle
Reflecting odds and evens
Yet holding on strong
Through the seasons
It's what keeps me breathing

Woman

I am versatile
In the spelling of my name
Though who I am always stays the same
I rock hard on this mic
Can't you feel the hype?
My prints on every page
You read as you travel on my stage
I am Mother Earth
You try to spit anger
And watch it reverse
Back at you
Cause that's not what you rehearsed
Your role is already scripted
Embedded and encrypted
You're just a prototype
That can be transferred and replaced
Saved on my hard drive and accidentally erased
I don't need you
You need me
I gave you the air that you breathe
Your knowledge and your seed
I gave you that high
You thought you got that from your weed
Please
I am your thought
Your fire and your desire
Go ahead try me if you think I'm a liar
You can't test something
That's already been tested
I'm positive I'm the best and
What I suggest is
You put in your resignation
Because I am
Woman.

Kiss of the roses

Remember I used to tell you to be careful out here?
You would suck your teeth and say, "I got this"
You ignored my warning
And went about your way
Until one day
You came and asked me for help
I helped you out and gave you a kiss
And said, "You have to be careful out here"
Once again my warning was ignored
And you went about your way
Sure enough I heard you scream for help
At which time I heard someone say
"Watch your back boy"
So I came to your rescue
And asked what's going on
You said, "Don't worry about it.
I got this"
So I gave you a kiss on the cheek
And let you go
On your way
Which was suppose to lead back to me, but
In due time I realized I'd lost you
You went the wrong way
I wish I'd never let you go, but
I told you to be careful.
And you didn't listen
Now it's too late
And all I can do now
Is kiss the roses.

Feast of Love

Today I fixed a big plate of love
With a side of affection
That was layered with kisses
I couldn't wait to serve this plate to him
I woke up this morning thinking
Tonight's the night
I had to make sure I fixed it right.
I made sure I put in all the
I, L, O, V, E, Y, O, U's in it
It was sweet to perfection!
And he loved it.

Masochism

I'm feeling it
Like needles sticking me
Thousands at a time
Feel like I fell on a porcupine
Feel like I'm slowly dying

I feel good.

I'm feeling it
Like a hard blow to my face
A thousand times over
Feel like I'm knocked unconscious
Feel like I'm slowly dying

I feel good.

I'm feeling it
Like laying in a hospital bed in pain
Except this time I am
I'm badly bruised
Feels like I'm slowly dying

But it feels good.

Black Love

He is the skin that covers my wounds
The air that surrounds the moon
I am his star
He is my night
He is the darkness on my plantains
That makes them so ripe and sweet
He is my eyes reflection
In the night when I sleep
He is the keys on my keyboard
That I love to stroke
He is the dots on my watch
And I am the hand that's on top of him every second and
Every hour in existence
I am his lighter
And he is my incense
He is the words on my page
That cannot be erased
And gets wiser with age
He is my BET
And my cup of tea
That I drink
As I sit here and think
About him whispering dirty little secrets
In my ear
Undressing my imagination
Arousing the sensations
Flowing through my veins
Causing the sensory nerves in my brain
To overload and explode
Into mental fragments of

Black love

Untitled

He whispered in my ear
So softly
His words sang a melody in my body
That made me quiver
It felt good
His hands gently massaging
My brown skin
Sending tickling sensations
Up and down my spine
Feeling soft blows
On my frontal lobe
He kisses me
My love begins to rain
I bleed impatient desire
He quickly fills me
And applies pressure
My heart beats faster
And faster
The pounding of his heart
Equivalent to his pounding thrusts
I feel the excitement building
The adrenaline rushing
He lets out a signal of release
I let out a sigh of relief
We stare deeply into each others eyes
And in a polite manner
I ask him, "What's your name?"

Life

Rested
I feel restless
Fearless
I feel fearful
Painless
I feel pain
Strong
I feel weak
Together
I feel apart
I'm hidden
But I stand before you

Tell Me Your Name

You should tell me your name
I see you every morning when you catch the train
With your suit and tie
That fits just right
Sexy dark brown eyes
That just hypnotizes me

You should tell me your name

You should tell me your name
Because we ride the same train
And share the same car
We get off at the same place
Besides you've already seen my face

You should tell me your name

You should tell me your name
And then I'll tell you mine
Then maybe go out
And have a good time
We'll keep in touch
With each other
We can be each other's lover
Come on
My sexy brother

Tell me your name

Tell me your name
Because I want you to
Tell me your name
Because I want you

Magic Moon

The light burns
From the night
Following my every move
A game of hide and seek
We play
From the back seat of the car
Standing still
It's the magic moon

Fallen Soldiers

Dear love,
We miss your smile
The letters you would send
Communicating with you
Through technology
Because you were so far away
Watching you watch your family via satellite
Seeing the expression on your face
We love you.

Dear strength,
Watching you fight a battle that's not your own
With such appreciation and dedication to your country
Clad with cowardice
You gave us a blanket of courage to
Not cry anymore, although
We miss you.

Dear fallen soldiers,
Communicating with you
Through time and space
Knowing you can see the expression on our faces
We send you smiles
And though we may not see you for a while
We love you
We miss you
And will never forget you!

Under the Bridge

Passerby's echo the frustrations of the world
Under the bridge
Tall tales of courage
Outpours from angry souls
Yet the toughest of them all still hide
Under the bridge
Grass roots & neo-souls speak words
In the form of hyperboles
Leaving actions hidden like water
Under the bridge

Haiku's

My deepest regret
Is that I wondered so long
About who I am

Now that I realize
Who I am, I can explore
What I was missing

And before life ends
I will make amends to those
Who I have wounded

And prepare myself
To shake the lord's hand after
My work here is done.

Dedication

I dedicate this book to my three closest friends, James, Jennine and Shomari, and my son Tyler Mitchell. They have given me so much love and support. I thank them for giving me the motivation and encouragement to fulfill my dream.

www.ingramcontent.com/pod-product-compliance
Ingram Content Group UK Ltd.
Pitfield, Milton Keynes, MK11 3LW, UK
UKHW041835200726
13854UKWH00003BA/1154